POEMS ABOUT MY LOCAL ASDA
and other suburban delights

By Jack Shamash

Illustrations by the author

William Cornelius Harris Publishing

In collaboration
with
London Poetry Books

ISBN 978-1-911232-58-2

William Young

34 Birchwood Close, Bordesley Road SM4 5NH

London Poetry Books

Dedicated to Carol and to the audiences at
The Poetry Shack

A nightmare

Southgate is under 20 foot of water,
The dams have burst.
Where shall we go?
Let us head to higher ground,
And take sanctuary in ASDA.
And while the waters are receding,
We can enjoy 'permanently lower prices forever'.

Fairtrade

At Asda there are packets of Fairtrade tea.
Note - they do not sell Un-Fairtrade tea,
Where the tea company pays with cheques that don't clear,
 Or with counterfeit notes.

Asda Fairtrade tea increases the sum of human happiness.
Oh envy the joyful grower bringing,
The fruits of his labour back to his smiling family!

Bag for life

Last night my wife and I went to Asda,
And - among other things -
spent eight pence on a Bag for Life.
The bag is guaranteed to last us a lifetime.
Every day we will look fondly at the bag,
And recall that evening,
All those years ago,
When we held hands and strolled through Asda,
Stocking up on milk, eggs and lightbulbs.

The side of the bag has the legend:
'If this bag breaks or gets damaged,
We will happily replace it free of charge.'
These little gestures give us peace of mind.
If I am involved in a horrific car crash or a dreadful fire,
My wife will be able to take the tattered shreds of the bag
And return them to Asda.
And the staff will give her a new bag,
And they will do this with smiles on their faces.
I sleep easy, knowing that whatever misfortunes may occur,
My wife and children will never be without a carrier bag.

The housewarming

To buy a housewarming present for a friend,
I went to the seasonal and garden section of Southgate Asda.
I found an attractive female garden gnome,
Wearing a blue bikini and carrying a seashell.
She had a saucy smile,
And - as garden gnomes go - looked quite sexy.
But I was concerned.
Would my friend think that I was having a joke,
Making an ironic comment on his poor taste,
Or his success with women?

I gave it some thought,
And went to the next aisle -
electrical and household goods -
Where I found a three-speed electric whisk.
Now he will have the lightest pancakes.
And the fluffiest sponges,
In the whole of N14!

The secrets of aisle 16

In ASDA I always go straight to aisle 16,
Which contains bicycle pumps,
Electrical screwdrivers and boxes of sockets for my car.
I do not have any immediate practical need for these items,
But I buy them to prove to myself,
That there is more to life,
Than simply pushing food into my
children's mouths.

The chiller unit

The chiller unit at the back of the store hums noisily.
It contains every variety of dairy produce,
Six types of milk, yoghurt in various flavours,
Mousse - chocolate and fruit -
Muller Rice with the funny corners,
Not to mention fromage frais, soured cream,
Double cream, single cream,
Whipping cream and creme fraiche.
The cows must be working overtime,
To stock the shelves at Southgate ASDA.

'Can't you see I'm busy?'

The aisle of spaghetti

Asda has tins of Tellytubby spaghetti
- with pasta shapes in rich tomato sauce.
It also has tins of Mutant Ninja Turtles spaghetti -
in rich tomato sauce,
Mr Tumble spaghetti in rich tomato sauce,
Angry Birds spaghetti, Hello Kitty spaghetti,
Minions spaghetti,
Thomas the Tank Engine spaghetti,
Even Star Wars spaghetti!
No-one can complain about a lack of variety,
In the tinned goods section of ASDA!

Easter Sunday
- Christ crucified,
resurrected and exalted at ASDA

The sun is shining, so why is ASDA closed?

And why is the car park empty?

It is the wish of the Lord!

For today is Easter Sunday.

On Good Friday Jesus was crucified,

But on Sunday he was resurrected.

So the store is closed.

And on Monday he is exalted,

And the store reopened.

Just in time for the sale of gardening sundries,

On the seasonal and fancy goods aisle in Southgate ASDA.

Asda's service team

Oh when I cannot find a till
Or cannot understand my bill,
Yes, these people are the cream!
Hail Asda's valiant service team!

They help me navigate the aisles,
They use their skills and native wiles,
They find me all the finest wines,
And show me all their latest lines.

If my footsteps start to slide
The service team will be my guide.
When I cannot find frozen peas
Thank God for people such as these.

And if perchance - and this is moot!
I bring back items that don't suit,
Or pay for something and they don't stock it,
They'll put the cash back in my pocket.

For them let's raise a hearty cheer,
At this and each oncoming year,
Our saviours, they deserve far more!
These unsung heroes of the store!

The tinned meat aisles

The tinned meat aisles of Asda are the land that
time forgot.
Skippers, sild, lump crab meat,
Who eats these things?
Or, for that matter, tinned cured chicken breasts,
Or chopped ham?

These are items that mothers might have sent their sons,
To cushion the loneliness of boarding school.
'I say, Mummy's sent me lunch tongue,
Lamb chunks in gravy,
Tinned peaches (semi-sweet) and condensed milk.'
Everything needed for midnight feasts in the dorm,
Curiously unappetising
But fervently desired.
Like cheaply-made Christmas presents
Or the cold kiss from a loveless mother.

Terror attack on ASDA

A notice on the door of Asda explains what to do
in event of armed attack,
'Run, Hide, Tell' - it announces.
When the gunman comes,
Get away from him as quickly as possible,
Turn your phone to silent and hide,
Call 999 to alert the police.
But under no circumstances,
Should you grab a stack of tablet computers,
And run off without paying.

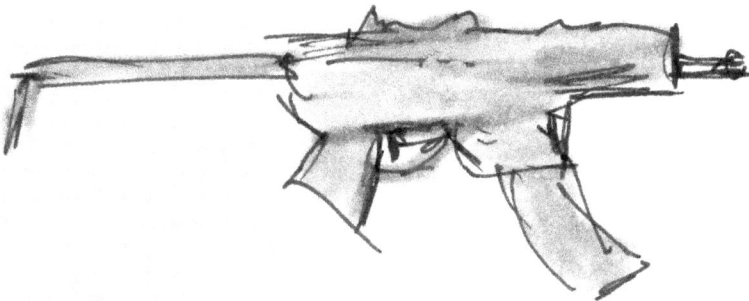

ASDA cereal

Up on the top floor of ASDA House,

The headquarters in the heart of Leeds,

The brightest graduates of their generation,

Are finding new names for the cereals at ASDA.

Malted Wheaties!

Cocosnaps!

The names come thick and fast.

Golden Balls, Blueberry Wheaties,

Chocoballs and Jungle Bites,

They pour out,

As enticing and sonorous,

As ASDA Choco Curls,

Cascading into a china breakfast bowl.

Halloween at Asda

On aisle 17 – 'Novelty and seasonal' –

There are all the items for Halloween.

It is £18 for a creepy costume,

£4 for a ghastly mask,

Another £4 for a horrid hat,

And £3 for dark make-up and fake blood.

For under £30 you can buy everything that you need,

To scare the wits out of little old ladies,

(while they proffer you bits of candy to make you go away).

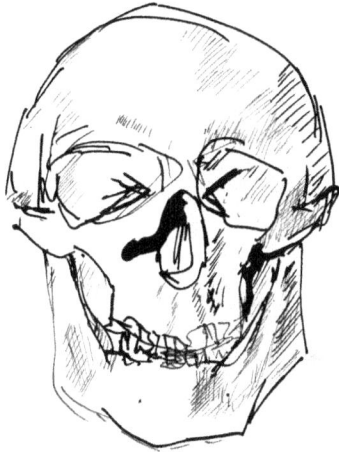

Words on a jacket

A woman is scrubbing the windows of ASDA,

With a large brush.

She has a slogan on her jacket,

'Cleaning your store all day everyday'.

Is this a proud boast,

Or a lament about the futility of working life?

Whatever - the windows are very clean,

And there is very little litter,

Blowing around in the parking lot.

The zombies at ASDA

At midnight
The lights dip,
The tills close,
And the staff at the check-outs clock off.
It is self service
Until 7.00am.

From now on,
ASDA is a land of zombies
And security guards
And staff stocking the shelves
For when the real people arrive.

Under the aisles

Beneath the ground at Southgate ASDA,
Can be heard,
The rumble of distant trains
This is the Piccadilly Line,
Carved out of the living rock,
By men with sinews of iron,
Stomachs like bands of steel,
And thighs like the trunks of trees.
If they were alive today,
They would buy the Asda meal deal,
Chicken salad on malted bread,
A diet coke and a bag of Walkers Crisps,
Enabling them to press on,
Digging without pause,
All the way from Oakwood to Cockfosters.

Bargain wings

My children are sick of chicken wings.

'We've had them three times this week,' they cry.

'Yes,' I tell them, 'But there is so much variety!

You can have them plain, with jerk seasoning,

Or with peri peri sauce.'

Still my children cry: 'We are sick of chicken wings.

Give us something else.'

'Are you crazy?' I say,

'With Asda chicken wings at £2.19 a kilo,

You will eat chicken wings until you start to fly'.

A dish of fish spunk

It is winter and I want something comforting for tea.
So I head to the fish counter at ASDA.
There is a blank-faced boy at the counter,
In a white coat and hat.
'Can I have some herring roe?' I say,
Pointing at a tray of pink slimy lumps.
He corrects me:
'It's not roe,' he tells me, 'It's milts.'
He has obviously been doing his homework.
And is not to be intimidated by a mere customer.
'Roe are the eggs of the fish,
Milts are fish sperm,' he says.
He looks me in the eye to emphasise his point,
'They are the sperm of the male herring.'
I look it up on Google,
Milts are indeed large clots of semen
That male herring discharge into the sea.
He is absolutely right.
Tonight I will consume fish cum on buttered toast.

'Skippers Brisling in Brine'

Buying sardines in olive oil,

I paused to look at a tin of 'Skippers Brisling in Brine'.

I know what brine is,

But what are 'skippers brisling'?

I look it up.

They are common sprats,

More properly 'sprattus sprattus',

And an offshoot of the herring family.

Such a humble fish!

And yet with a noble lineage,

And such a distinguished name!

Launceston

Standing on top of Launceston Castle in Cornwall,

I wave down to my kids,

Who are standing at the base of the castle.

I wonder: 'What do they think of me?

Do they think: that's the nicest man on earth?

Do they feel great waves of warmth?

Or do they think:

'That's just Dad wandering around old ruins,

Being boring about architecture'?

Perhaps they think: 'I hate that man!

How convenient it would be if he fell down the castle steps,

And landed in a sticky pile by the outer bailey.

If he fell, my friends would feel sorry for me,

I would get lots of presents,

And I'd have a new dad,

Preferably with a bit more money,

And a better sense of humour.'

Whatever their thoughts,

They keep them to themselves,

But stare up through the castle railings,

Wave their comics at me and smile.

There are no buttons on my coat

There are no buttons on my coat,
And when the wind blows I get wet,
And when the sun shines I forget,
There are no buttons on my coat.

I have got myself a girl,
Yet I'm as miserable as sin,
Because my coat is all done in,
There are no buttons on my coat.

Water soaks into my feet,
I watch drizzle in the street,
I stand and watch the fag ends float,
The buttons falling off my coat.

I'll eat a sandwich drenched in rain,
I'll grasp the nettle by the throat,
And sew the buttons on my coat
And try to make it good again.

One day when I earn some more
I'll buy myself a button jar,
And drive around in my new car,
Dispensing buttons to the poor.

On my nose there is a drip,
I don't think poverty is hip,
It really gets my bloody goat,
There are no buttons on my coat.

The ambulance poem

God bless you little ambulance,
God speed you to the scene,
It doesn't matter if you're poor,
Or if you are a queen.

But if you have an accident,
Or a heart attack,
You'll take me to hospital,
And you'll bring me back.

While policemen take particulars,
And firemen stop and stare,
It's nice to see an ambulance,
And know that people care.

My father's penis

My father's penis was much loved,
God bless my father's penis,
It was our family's pride and joy,
The brightest and the cleanest.

His wondrous member was strong veined,
The joy it gave was quite unfeigned,
Our family lineage it maintained,
It was a noble object.

His lustre now is somewhat dimmed,
His nether quarters rarely rimmed,
Yet stands above all lesser tools,
The sceptre of our family jewels.

He ruled us with his rod of iron,
He had the bollocks of a lion,
Oh, how I wish that they were mine,
God bless my father's penis.

My pencil

Oh my dear old little pencil,

I have almost eaten you,

Your writing days are finished,

Though you are so good to chew.

But I can't stand the little splinters,

They get stuck in my maw,

But it's something I'll put up with,

'Cause that's what friends are for.

I will crack your brittle lead,

I will suck your bitter sap,

I will clutch you to my bosom,

I will sit you on my lap.

Though you cannot write a letter,

And your shiny paint is gone,

I will love you little pencil,

As I did when you were young.

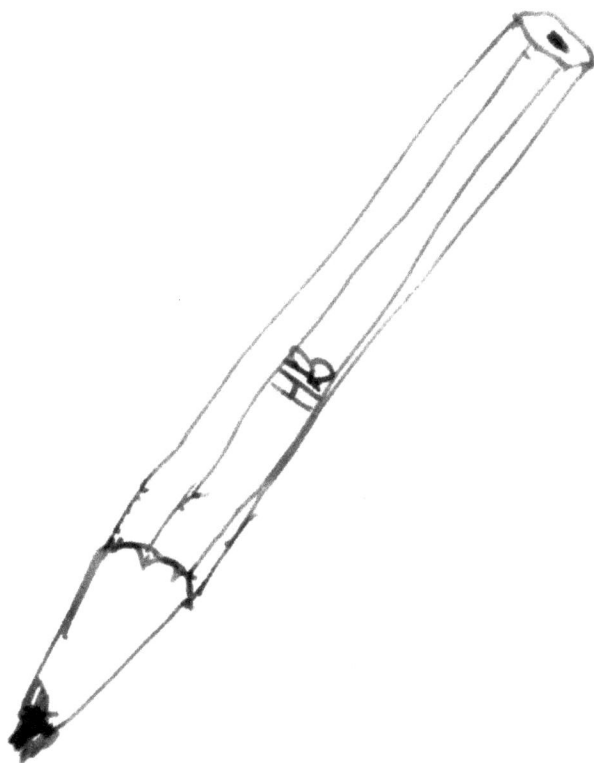

The workers

My wife cooks for me,

She cooks for me in a workman-like way,

After all, she is my wife,

I cannot expect cordon bleu cooking,

Not on a daily basis.

I make love to my wife,

I make love to my wife in a workman-like way,

After all, she is my wife,

She cannot expect cordon bleu sex,

Not on a daily basis.

You have to take the rough with the smooth,

Married life is not a dinner party,

Or a cocaine binge,

Or one long fortnight in Florida,

In the honeymoon suite,

With a Jacuzzi and choice of gourmet sandwiches.

You have to work at a relationship,

To keep things together,

Before you get down to the fancy stuff,

There's meat to be put on the table.

Teddies for the dead

The dead have their own teddy bears,
Clinging to railings by the roadside,
With posies of decayed flowers
In yellowed cellophane wrappers.

The teddy bears all cry: 'Play with me,'
But despite the pleading plastic eyes,
And outstretched arms, nobody will.
They know that these teddies belong to the dead.

One day at the time of resurrection,
These teddies will walk again.
United with their owners,
Pure and whole once more.

But for now they cling,
Silent against their railings,
Wishing they could be in the arms of someone
            who loved them,
And wondering what they've done to deserve this.

The flies in Cannes

After half a lifetime
I returned to the South of France,
And nothing has changed.
The files that bite me now
Are the same flies that bit me 30 years ago.
I recognise some of the flies,
They are old, fatter and more sluggish,
They have experienced the world.
And because they are mature and used to finer foods,
My blood lacks the savour that it once had for them.
These are well-bred flies,
Who whine in complaint,
Pat their well-rounded stomachs,
And leer at the female flies.
They dine in the kitchens in the Martinez,
 And spend their days at the beach.
Even though – at this time of year -
The beaches are crowded with other flies.
They like the Martinez,
The food is good,
And they believe it is worth a little sacrifice,
If you can get a nice table with a good view of the sea.

The voice of the cactus

This is the voice of the cactus,

I heard when my mother whacked us,

It says, 'No water in winter,

Or I'll give you a cactus splinter.'

It says: 'I like warm places,

Give or I smash your faces,

Not too near the radiator,

Or you'll hear from the cactus later.'

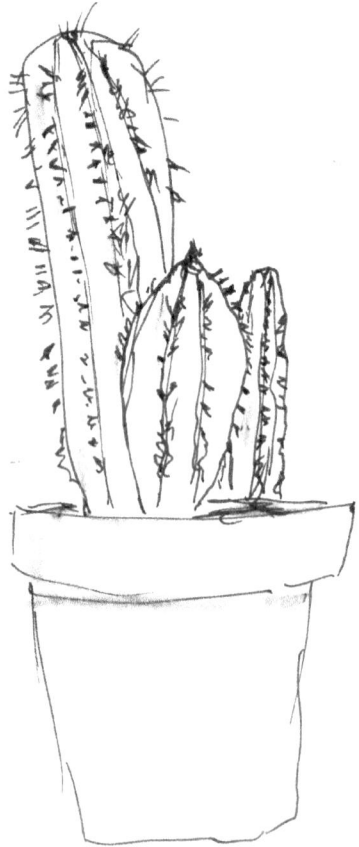

Little wart

I do not like you little wart,
You do not do the things you ought,
You come whether I want or no,
And resolute refuse to go.

Salactol cream or heated brand,
Will not remove you from my hand,
Immune from chemical attack,
You always seem to come right back.

Grate it, slash it, slice its heart,
It shows no readiness to part.
Will you leave us? You will not!
I wish that you'd clear out damned spot!

Whenever excised, charmed or filed,
That little warty lump runs wild,
And so, in sum, perhaps it's best,
To leave it, an unwelcome guest.

From a train window

Once, on a golden sunlit evening,

I looked out the window of a Piccadilly line train,

To see,

Beyond the large hedge at the end of the bowling green,

A young couple making love.

The boy was around twenty, his girlfriend, slightly younger,

Sitting on top of him with her skirt around her waist:

An attractive Asian girl with long black hair,

And delicate white knickers.

Perhaps I should have called the police on my mobile.

Perhaps I should have been angry -

Contacted the council and complained about the misuse of

public space.

But all I could feel was jealousy.

Wishing I was twenty again, with a girl astride me,

Feeling the grass on my back and the sun on my brow,

Rather than sitting in a tube train, in a tight suit,

And not a pair of white knickers in sight.

Underpants

Every morning I get out of bed,
And take off the underpants of yesterday,
And put on the underpants of today.
This simple act,
I see as a metaphor for change and renewal.
I try to explain this to my wife but she will have none of it.
'Shut up with your metaphors,' she says,
'And put your bloody undies in the laundry.'

The Mouse

That little mouse stuck in my trap,

Nibbling the chocolate button I have left there,

How long will it take before it learns that -

despite appearances -

There is no such thing as a free lunch?

King Charles' prostate cancer
– lines in thanks for his recovery

Charles stands above the royal bowl,
Yet he cannot reach his goal.
Something is amiss,
With the fountain of the regal piss.

There's a blockage in the royal flow
The doctors say it has to go:
'The dribbling winkle of the king
Will soon be a bygone thing
We will improve his erection
with a trans-urethral resection.'

The doctors stopped him getting iller
Which was a great relief to Camilla.
A nation rejoices once again,
His urine flows like summer rain,
So one big hand for Charlie's gland,
The noblest prostate in the land.

COME BACK SOON

You can follow Jack Shamash on Facebook and The Poetry
Shack on Facebook and Instagram